HABARI GANI?

(How are you?)

MAMA, BABA AND MPENDWA!

(Loved ones)

We created My Daddy Loves Me to celebrate all the Black fathers who take care of their children and show them love on a daily basis. Mainstream media, society and schools often depict Black fathers and our sons in a negative way. It is our responsibility to counter this misinformation by celebrating the many Black men who willingly go above and beyond in their duties to support, love and protect their children. Today and every day, we salute those fathers and encourage them to keep up the good work!

With all our hearts, we believe Black fathers have to be intentional in and conscious of how we show our sons love. If they are to be shielded from the negativity that paints them as less than, we, Black fathers, must utilize every opportunity to show and tell our sons we love them.

We must not reserve our expressions of love for our biological sons only, but also extend it to our friends' sons, nephews, neighborhood boys, and any other Black boys we encounter. They are all our cultural sons. They are all our responsibility.

Black fathers have a unique and particular responsibility to do for our sons what no one else can. We have to stick together and work together to raise our children and hold each other accountable for our words and actions. Though we are busy with work, life and other responsibilities, our duty to our children remains unchanged. We must let nothing stop us from showing our children love, spending time with them, and exposing them to culturally uplifting experiences. Remember, you are a great father and our children need you!

WE HOPE YOU ENJOY THE STORY!

SEKO

One day, Daddy and Sekou were sitting in his room, reading a book. As Daddy read, Sekou looked up at him and asked, "Do you love me, Daddy?"

Malcolm X

Dr. Martin Luther King, Jr

Marcus Garvey

Black Child's Pledge

Daddy stopped reading and looked down at Sekou. "Yes, I love you."

"Why do you love me, Daddy?" asked Sekou, staring into his father's eyes.

Daddy thought about Sekou's question briefly and then replied, "I love you because you are my son, and I am so happy that God blessed Mommy and I to have you. And guess what," he said, smiling.

Malcolm X

Black Cl

"What, Daddy? Sekou responded, as his eyes sparkled with excitement.

"Did you know I loved you before you were born?"

"Really!" Sekou said. He wasn't even sure how that could be possible. "Did you really love me before I was born?" he asked, a tad curious.

Daddy laughed. "Yes, sir. I use to lie on Mommy's tummy and talk to you while you were still in her womb. I wondered what you would look like and how you would sound."

"Really, Daddy?" said Sekou excitedly.

He imagined being in Mommy's belly and hearing Daddy's deep, familiar voice.

Yes, really. I remember the day you were born, when the doctor brought you out of mommy's tummy. I was so happy! I didn't want to leave your side," Daddy explained, reminiscing on that beautiful day.

"You were happy when I was born?" Sekou asked with a big smile. He liked to hear Daddy's stories.

Yes, I was. I held your little hand for the first time while the nurse gave you your checkup. She even let me help. Afterwards, we took you to Mommy's hospital room to see her," explained Daddy.

"You helped give me my first checkup! So you're like a doctor?" Sekou asked excitedly.

Daddy laughed. "Well, I'm not exactly a doctor that works in a hospital, but I am a doctor. As much as I loved you then, I love you even more now. My love for you has grown over time," Daddy said.

Grown? How? Sekou asked. He didn't know love could grow.

"As I spend time with you and watch you grow older, I find so many more things to love about you," replied Daddy.

"Like what?" inquired Sekou. He wanted to know more about what his father loved about him.

Daddy thought for a second. There were so many things he loved. "Well, I love it when you call me Daddy. It makes me feel so good inside. I am both honored and humbled to be your father because it is a big responsibility," he said.

Sekou smiled and said, "I love calling you Daddy! I want to be just like you when I grow up." He imagined himself as a man, strong and smart, just like Daddy.

W hat else do you love about me? asked Sekou. He wanted to know more.

"I love to see you playing with your toy cars, without a care in the world.

Your innocence shines through," said Daddy.

"I like cars, Daddy!" said Sekou. He glanced over at the big red one on his bed.

I know you do. I really love playing cars and spending time with you, Sekou. I also love talking to you and taking you outside to ride your bike around our neighborhood. I love everything we do together," Daddy said.

"I like riding my bike!" shouted Sekou.

addy continued. "I love it when you lie next to me on the couch and we somehow always end up falling asleep together." He gave Sekou's back a gentle rub.

"I like sleeping next to you too, Daddy," said Sekou.

And even though I'm really tired most times and haven't fully woken up yet, I like it when you wake me in the morning to read you a book," said Daddy.

"I wake you up because I love the way you read me stories. You make the books so fun," Sekou said.

"I am happy you like the way I read to you," Daddy said. It felt good to get his son's stamp of approval.

Stories help me learn new things, Daddy, and you know how much I love learning," explained Sekou.

"I know you do. That's why I love taking you and picking you up from school on the train," said Daddy.

I love taking the train to school with you too, Daddy. I really like it when you read the train safety instruction manual to me," exclaimed Sekou.

"I'm surprised you like it when I read the instruction manual. I like it even more when you read to me." Daddy said proudly.

Daddy got a thoughtful look on his face before he continued. "The main reason I love you is because you are a gift from God, and you bring out the best in me as a man and a father. I have a responsibility to teach you how to be a man and a father. I take that responsibility very seriously."

Sekou leaned on Daddy's shoulder. "I learn a lot from the example you set for me every day. I want to make you proud of me," he said.

I am already proud of you, Sekou, Daddy said with his face beaming. "And I know you will continue to make me proud as you develop into a man."

He gave Sekou a hug and a kiss. "I love you, son," he said. "And I love you too, Daddy," said Sekou.

A ll of a sudden, they heard Mommy yelling from
the bottom of the stairs.

"Sekou!" she said.

"Yes, Mommy," Sekou yelled back.

"What are you doing?" she replied.

I 'm upstairs in my room with Daddy, yelled Sekou.
Daddy gave Sekou a gentle push.

"Sekou, go see what
Mommy wants."

"Ok, Daddy," he said,
standing to go
downstairs.

Mommy, did you want me? he asked when he got to the bottom of the stairs. "Oh, I didn't want anything, Sekou. I just wanted to know what you were doing," she said with a warm smile.

"I was upstairs reading a book and talking to Daddy. Hey, Mommy, did you know Daddy loves me?" asked Sekou. This was exciting news that he had to share.

Mommy laughed. "Of course, I do, Sekou. Your Daddy loves you a whole lot and he loves me too!" she said.

Sekou smiled and said to himself,

MY DADDY ♥ ME!!

Feeling loved, he went back upstairs to finish reading his story with Daddy.

CULTURALLY UPLIFTING FAMILY WORK!

Black Families should engage regularly in culturally uplifting learning activities that strengthen and help our families learn and experience new things together. We humbly present these culturally uplifting learning activities for you to engage in by yourself as well as with your biological and cultural sons:

1. Self-Assessment: Think about the ways you show your son love. Do your ways of showing love represent how you want your son to experience your love? Do you show your love explicitly (clear and obvious) or implicitly (not stated)? How does your son know you love him? Reflect on these questions. Make sure you show your son love in your own special way.

2. Tell your son you love him on a daily basis. Don't wait for a special occasion.

3. Read your son a book daily that positively depicts Black boys, families and children. Discuss the book with him.

4. Become active in your son's school to develop relationships with his teachers, administrators, other school officials and parents. This will also allow you to develop relationship with your son's friends and other young men in the school so that you can positively shape their academic and social development, too.

5. Volunteer regularly in male mentoring, afterschool, Saturday school, and/or summer school programs to spend time with your biological and cultural sons.

6. Read books geared toward Black men raising Black boys (and girls) for ideas about how to support their social, intellectual and cultural development. Following is a list of resources:

- **The Warrior Method: A Parent's Guide to Rearing Healthy Black Boys** by Raymond Winbush
- **Raising Black Boys** by Jawanza Kunjufu
- **Promise Kept: Raising Black Boys to Succeed in School and Life** by Joe Brewster, Michele Stephenson and Hilary Beard
- **Motivating Black Males to Achieve in School and Life** by Baruti Kalefe
- **Visions for Black Men** by Na'im Akbar
- **Raising Him Alone** by David Miller and Matthew P. Stevens
- **Tough Notes: A Healing Call for Creating Exceptional Black Men** by Haki Madhubuti
- **Black Men Obsolete, Single, Dangerous? The Afrikan American Family in Transition** by Haki Madhubuti
- **The Conspiracy to Destroy Black Boys** by Jawanza Kunjufu

ABOUT THE AUTHORS

The Sekou Family is a Black family that lives in Baltimore, Maryland. They believe in the importance of Black families and children connecting, honoring and respecting our cultural heritage and traditions in Africa, America, the Caribbean, and the Diaspora. As a family, we work hard to learn about our cultural heritage and traditions. We practice the Nguzo Saba (The 7 Principles of Blackness) in our everyday lives and give back to our community.

The stories presented in our books are fictionalized accounts based on real events in our family and our journey to live a life that connects, honors, and respects our cultural heritage and traditions. Reading should be a regular occurrence in Black families, and it is important for Black children to see images that look like them in the books they read.

Becoming parents and watching our son, Sekou, grow up inspired these books and the stories in them. Sekou is co-author because he has contributed greatly to the books. Mama and Baba use his name as co-authors of the books to honor his contributions. We use Afrika as our last name to represent our quest to positively uplift our cultural heritage and traditions originating in Africa. Sekou has inspired us to live a life that more closely reflects our beliefs and political ideology. We strongly believe we have to create Black institutions to positively uplift Black families and children, and connect them to their cultural heritage and traditions.

Baba Sekou Afrika, Ed.D. (also known as Julius Davis) is an assistant professor of mathematics education at Bowie State University. His scholarship and advocacy focuses on the intellectual and social development of Black boys and young men. He has studied and traveled to Malawi, Tanzania, and Ethiopia on the continent of Africa to learn more about our cultural heritage and traditions.

Mama Sekou Afrika (also known as Yolanda Davis) is a clinical research professional who has studied and traveled to Senegal on the continent of Africa and the Caribbean Islands to learn more about our cultural heritage and traditions.

Sekou Afrika (also known as Sekou Davis) is a student at Ujamaa Shule, the oldest independent Afrikan School in the United States. He plays the Afrikan drums with his brothers and sisters at Ujamaa. To start his formal school-based academic and social development, Sekou attended Watoto Development Center in Baltimore, MD, an Afrikan-centered institution.

Asante Sana (Thank you very much) for practicing Ujamaa (cooperative economics) by purchasing this book and supporting our Black-owned family business. A portion of the proceeds from this book will be used to support and sponsor efforts to culturally uplift Black children and families.

Your Support is Greatly Appreciated!

Baba Sekou Afrika, Mama Sekou Afrika, Sekou Afrika

KISWAHILI GLOSSARY

We believe Black families and children should learn one or more African languages that reflect our culture and traditions before learning foreign languages that reflect other ethnic groups' cultures and traditions. As a family, we are learning **Kiswahili**, a language spoken across many countries on continent of Africa. It is our hope and desire that more Black families and children will learn to speak Kiswahili. We invite you to learn Kiswahili with us:

Jambo – Hello

Asante Sana – Thank you very much

Baba – Father

Mama – Mother

Watoto – Children

Habari gani – How are you?

Nzuri na wewe je – Fine, and you?

Ninakupenda – I love you

Mpendwa – Loved ones

Nguzo Saba – The seven principles of Blackness.

Kujichagulia – Self-determination. It is one of the seven principles of Blackness.

Kuumba – Creativity. It is one of the seven principles of Blackness.

Ujamaa – Cooperative economics. It is one of the seven principles of Blackness.

KUJICHAGULIA PRESS

We define, speak and create for ourselves to celebrate our African and African American cultural heritage and uplift our people using our Kuumba (creativity).

Text copyright 2016 by Kujichagulia Press
Illustration copyright 2016
All rights reserved. Published by Kujichagulia Press

Title: My Daddy Loves Me / Written by:
Baba Sekou Afrika, Mama Sekou Afrika, and Sekou Afrika
Illustrated By: Eloy Claudio
Edited By: Nadirah Angail
Book Design By: Eloy Claudio

Summary: The book is about how a Black father shares his love for his son. It celebrates

Black fathers who take care of their children and show them love on a daily basis.

ISBN-13: 978-0996459501
ISBN-10: 0996459502

For more information or to book an event,
contact Baba/Mama Sekou at books@kujichaguliapress.com.
Kujichagulia Press
P.O. Box 31766
Baltimore, MD
www.kujichaguliapress.com

 KujichaguliaPress   KujichaguliaPress   @Kujichaguliaprs

#MyDaddyLoves
#ILoveMySon

Manufactured by Amazon.ca
Bolton, ON

16529095R00019